HOW TO WIN AN ELECTION

HOW TO WIN
AN ELECTION

■ ■ ■ ■ ■

An Ancient Guide for Modern Politicians

Quintus Tullius Cicero

Translated and with an introduction by
Philip Freeman

PRINCETON UNIVERSITY PRESS

PRINCETON AND OXFORD

Published by Princeton University Press, 41 William Street,
Princeton, New Jersey 08540
In the United Kingdom: Princeton University Press, 6 Oxford Street,
Woodstock, Oxfordshire OX20 1TW

press.princeton.edu

Library of Congress Cataloging-in-Publication Data
Cicero, Quintus Tullius.
[Commentariolum petitionis. English]
How to win an election : an ancient guide for modern politicians /
Quintus Tullius Cicero ; translated and with an introduction by
Philip Freeman
p.   cm.
Includes bibliographical references and index.
ISBN 978-0-691-15408-4 (hardcover : acid-free paper)
I. Freeman, Philip, 1961- II. Title.
PA6371.C4A24 2011
324.7'20937—dc23
2011034838

British Library Cataloging-in-Publication Data is available

This book has been composed in Garamond and Futura

Printed on acid-free paper. ∞

Printed in the United States of America

1 3 5 7 9 10 8 6 4 2

CONTENTS

INTRODUCTION

In the summer of 64 BC, Marcus Tullius Cicero, the greatest orator ancient Rome ever produced, was running for consul, the highest office in the Roman Republic. He was forty-two years old, the son of a wealthy businessman from the small town of Arpinum south of Rome. His father had seen that Marcus and his younger brother Quintus received the finest education and had even sent the boys to Greece to study with the most noted philosophers and orators of the day.

Marcus was a gifted speaker and possessed a brilliant mind equal to his golden tongue. What he lacked was the advantage of noble birth. Ancient Roman society was highly class-conscious and dismissed men such as Marcus Cicero as unfit to preside over the republic. He was determined to prove them wrong.

As a young man Marcus had completed an undistinguished year in military service under the father of the future Roman general Pompey the Great, who would one day defend the state against Julius Caesar. This younger Pompey became a patron of Marcus and helped him in his subsequent political career. At twenty-five, Marcus won his first case in the Roman courts defending a well-connected man against murder charges. His reputation grew in the years to follow as he successfully represented many prominent men—victories that also helped him rise through the political ranks of the republic. He had already served admirably in the important but lesser offices of quaestor and praetor. However, no man outside the noble families had been elected as a consul for thirty years, making the attainment of this ultimate goal by Marcus unlikely.

Yet in 64, the other candidates for the consulship—most notably Antonius (known as Hybrida) and Catiline—were such an unsavory lot that some of the nobility held their noses and threw their support behind Marcus Cicero. Still, the thought of an outsider from a small town being one of the two consuls to govern the ancient republic, ruler of millions across the Mediterranean lands, was too much for many of the blue-blooded families to stomach. Marcus was going to have a long and difficult campaign if he was going to win.

At this point the more practical Quintus decided that his elder brother needed some advice. Quintus was four years younger than Marcus, with a fiery and sometimes cruel temperament. Although overshadowed by his elder sibling, he was fiercely loyal to Marcus and recognized that his brother's success would pave his own way to fame and fortune. He had even married the headstrong Pomponia, sister of Marcus's best friend Atticus, and fathered a son with her two years earlier, though the marriage was always rocky.

As the campaign for consul was beginning, Quintus wrote a short pamphlet to Marcus on electioneering in the form of a letter. The result is a little-known text that has somehow survived the centuries, called in Latin the *Commentariolum Petitionis*. Some specialists in Roman literature doubt that Quintus wrote the work, believing it was another contemporary or perhaps a

Roman from the following century. Others would agree that Quintus was indeed the author. What matters, however, is not the identity of the writer but what he says. The author was clearly someone intimately familiar with Roman politics in the first century BC who possessed a keen sense of how elections are won in any age.

Rome in the days of the Cicero brothers was a vast empire run as if it were still a small town nestled among seven hills along the Tiber River. Politics was deeply personal, controlled by a few leading families of the city, and centered around the Roman Forum, a former swamp in the center of town. Although Roman citizens lived across the Mediterranean region, there was no such thing as an absentee ballot. All campaigning was done by candidates within the city of Rome or in nearby towns.

Any Roman who aspired to the consulship was required, after obligatory military service, to be elected first to a series of lower offices known as the *cursus honorum*, or "path of honors." The first step in this long process was to be chosen around the age of thirty as one of the quaestors elected each year to manage the mundane tasks of governance, such as running the treasury. Service as a praetor came next, and brought with it such responsibilities as managing the courts, after which a man might be sent abroad to govern a Roman province. Only a few would choose to campaign for the ultimate prize, the office of consul. These two annual magistrates held supreme executive power over the republic and were responsible for both civil and military affairs. Election to the consulship was jealously guarded by the aristocracy of Rome, for service in this highest office granted a man and his descendants the coveted status of nobility.

The Romans scoffed at the Greek idea of "one man, one vote" as an invitation to mob rule. Any adult male citizen could cast a ballot, but this was done in a complicated system of groups. Individuals helped determine how their own group would vote, but it was the group itself that cast a single vote within the assembly. These groups might be military in origin (centuries) or tribal, but by the time of Cicero their original significance had been replaced by class designations based on wealth. The richest citizens held a disproportionate degree of power over the much more numerous lower classes. Often a sufficient number of ballots would be cast to elect a candidate even before the poorer citizens could come to the polls. The system also favored those who lived in or near Rome, since voting had to be done in person. A farmer or merchant of modest income living far from the city was unlikely to make the journey to cast his ballot.

Yet for those citizens who lived in the capital or had the means to travel to Rome for elections, the process of choosing consuls was orderly and usually fair, in spite of the rampant bribery and occasional violence of the campaigns. Citizens would gather early in the morning on the nearby Campus Martius to hear final speeches, then divide into their centuries in roped-off areas to cast their votes. Voting was by secret ballot, as each man wrote the name of his favored candidate on a small wax-covered wooden tablet and placed it in a large wickerwork basket. The votes of each group were announced as soon as they were tabulated. The first candidate to achieve a majority according to the system was declared the winner, with the man placing second in the polls named as the junior consul. The senior consul could then take up the *fasces*—a bundle of rods with an axe fixed in the top symbolizing his authority—on his inauguration day on January 1 and for one year enjoy the unmatched power and prestige of governing the Roman Republic, whose might extended over much of the known world.

Understanding the basics of the Roman electoral system in the first century BC is useful for appreciating the advice Marcus Cicero receives in this letter, but the real pleasure for most modern readers is its unashamedly pragmatic advice on how to manipulate voters and win political office.

Like Machiavelli's *Prince*, this short treatise provides timeless and no-nonsense counsel to those who aspire to power. Idealism and naïveté are left by the wayside as Quintus tells his brother—and all of us—how the down-and-dirty business of successful campaigning really works.

The letter is full of priceless advice for modern candidates, but some of the choicest gems are:

1. *Make sure you have the backing of your family and friends.* Loyalty begins at home. If your spouse and children aren't behind you, not only will you have a hard time winning but it will look bad to voters. And as Quintus warns his brother, the most destructive rumors about a candidate begin among those closest to him.

2. *Surround yourself with the right people.* Build a talented staff you can trust. You can't be everywhere at once, so find those who will represent you as if they were trying to be elected themselves.

3. *Call in all favors.* It's time to gently (or not so gently) remind everyone you have ever helped that they owe you. If someone isn't under obligation to you, let them know that their support now will put you in their debt in the future. And as an elected official, you will be well placed to help them in their time of need.

4. *Build a wide base of support.* For Marcus Cicero this meant appealing primarily to the traditional power brokers both in the Roman Senate and the wealthy business community—no easy task since these groups were often at odds with each

other. But Quintus urges his brother as an outsider in the political game to go further and win over the various special interest groups, local organizations, and rural populations ignored by other candidates. Young voters should be courted as well, along with anyone else who might be of use. As Quintus notes, even people no decent person would associate with in normal life should become the closest of friends during a campaign if they can help get you elected. Restricting yourself to a narrow base of support guarantees failure.

But how do you win over such a wide array of voters?

5. *Promise everything to everybody.* Except in the most extreme cases, candidates should say whatever the particular

crowd of the day wants to hear. Tell traditionalists you have consistently supported conservative values. Tell progressives you have always been on their side. After the election you can explain to everyone that you would love to help them, but unfortunately circumstances beyond your control have intervened. Quintus assures his brother that voters will be much angrier if he refuses to promise them their hearts' desire than if he backs out later.

6. *Communication skills are key.* In ancient Rome the art of public speaking was studied diligently by all men who aspired to political careers. In spite of the new and varied forms of media today, a poor communicator is still unlikely to win an election.

7. *Don't leave town.* In Marcus Cicero's day this meant sticking close to Rome. For

modern politicians it means being on the ground pressing the flesh wherever the key voters are at a particular moment. There is no such thing as a day off for a serious candidate. You can take a vacation after you win.

8. *Know the weaknesses of your opponents—and exploit them.* Just as Quintus takes a hard look at those running against his brother, all candidates should do an honest inventory of both the vulnerabilities and strengths of their rivals. Winning candidates do their best to distract voters from any positive aspects of their opponents possess by emphasizing the negatives. Rumors of corruption are prime fodder. Sexual scandals are even better.

9. *Flatter voters shamelessly.* Marcus Cicero was always courteous, but he could be formal and distant. Quintus warns him

that he needs to warm up to voters. Look them in the eye, pat them on the back, and tell them they matter. Make voters believe you genuinely care about them.

10. *Give people hope.* Even the most cynical voters want to believe in someone. Give the people a sense that you can make their world better and they will become your most devoted followers—at least until after the election, when you will inevitably let them down. But by then it won't matter because you will have already won.

There are many other useful bits of advice in the letter that modern readers can happily discover for themselves. Even though the Roman Republic vanished over two thousand years ago, it is fascinating to see that the more things change, the more they stay the same.

And you might be wondering how the election for consul turned out. Did Marcus beat the odds and win his campaign? Did the advice of Quintus work? What became of the two brothers after the election? Read on and at the end of the letter discover what happened.

A NOTE ON THE TRANSLATION

Translating the text of the *Commentariolum Petitionis* is no easy task. The Latin is at times obscure, while the manuscripts passed down to us have been corrupted at several points. I have tried to make my translation accessible, colloquial, and as clear as possible to modern readers, while remaining faithful to the sense of the original text.

There is also the problem of Roman social and political vocabulary. Many of the Latin terms have no clear equivalent in modern languages. The Latin *equites*, for example, literally means "horsemen" and reflects an origin in cavalry service. Because of this it is often translated as "knights"—but for most readers this evokes a misleading image of King Arthur and his Round Table. In Cicero's time the designation of *equites* had moved far beyond a connection to horses and referred instead to the social class of moderately wealthy citizens just below senators, to whose ranks they could rise as Cicero did. Most of them were businessmen, so I have used the term "business community" or similar in my translation. Likewise for the diverse social groups of *sodalitates* or *collegia*: I have used terms such as "organizations" or "special interest groups" that best approximate their role in first-century BC Rome. For the Latin *optimates* and *populares*—literally, "best men" and "men of the people"—I have respectively used the terms "traditionalists" and "populists" since these would be the closest modern equivalents. I refer readers to the glossary for a more detailed explanation of these and other terms.

HOW TO WIN AN ELECTION

COMMENTARIOLUM PETITIONIS

Quintus Marco Fratri:*

1. Etsi tibi omnia suppetunt ea quae consequi ingenio aut usu homines aut diligentia possunt, tamen amore nostro non sum alienum arbitratus ad te perscribere ea quae mihi veniebant in mentem dies ac noctes de petitione tua cogitanti, non ut aliquid ex his novi addisceres, sed ut ea quae in re dispersa atque infinita viderentur esse ratione et distributione sub uno aspectu ponerentur.

2. Civitas quae sit cogita, quid petas, qui sis. Prope cotidie tibi hoc ad Forum

---

*Latin text © Oxford University Press. M. Tulli Ciceronis, *Epistulae* vol. 3. edited by L. C. Purser, Oxford: Clarendon Press, 1953.

HOW TO WIN AN ELECTION

To my brother Marcus,

1. Although you already have all the skills a man can possess through natural ability, experience, and hard work, because of the affection we have for one another I would like to share with you what I have been thinking about night and day concerning your upcoming campaign. It's not that you need my advice, but such affairs can seem so chaotic that it's sometimes best to lay things out in one place in a logical order.

2. Always remember what city this is, what office it is you seek, and who you are. Every day as you go down to the Forum, you should say to yourself: "I am

descendenti meditandum est: "Novus sum, consulatum peto, Roma est."

Nominis novitatem dicendi gloria maxime sublevabis. Semper ea res plurimum dignitatis habuit. Non potest qui dignus habetur patronus consularium indignus consulatu putari. Quam ob rem quoniam ab hac laude proficisceris et quicquid es ex hoc es, ita paratus ad dicendum venito quasi in singulis causis iudicium de omni ingenio futurum sit.

3. Eius facultatis adiumenta, quae tibi scio esse seposita, ut parata ac prompta sint cura, et saepe quae de Demosthenis studio et exercitatione scripsit Demetrius recordare, deinde ut amicorum et multitudo et genera appareant. Habes enim ea quae

an outsider. I want to be a consul. This is Rome."

Any criticism of your outsider status will be greatly mitigated by your well-known skill as a speaker, for oratory has always been highly valued. After all, anyone who is good enough to defend former consuls in court should be worthy to be a consul himself. Since you are such an excellent communicator and your reputation has been built on this fact, you should approach every speaking engagement as if your entire future depended on that single event.

3. It is crucial that you take stock of the many advantages you possess—read what Demetrius wrote about the study and practice of Demosthenes. Consider that few outsiders have the number and variety of supporters that you do. All those holding

non multi homines novi habuerunt, omnis publicanos, totum fere equestrem ordinem, multa propria municipia, multos abs te defensos homines cuiusque ordinis, aliquot collegia, praeterea studio dicendi concili-atos plurimos adulescentulos, cotidianam amicorum adsiduitatem et frequentiam.

4. Haec cura ut teneas commonendo et rogando et omni ratione efficiendo ut intellegant qui debent tua causa, referendae gratiae, qui volunt, obligandi tui tempus sibi aliud nullum fore. Etiam hoc multum videtur adiuvare posse novum hominem, hominum nobilium voluntas et maxime consularium. Prodest quorum in locum

public contracts are on your side, as well as most of the business community. The Italian towns also support you. Don't forget about all the people you have successfully defended in court, clients from a wide variety of social backgrounds. And, of course, remember the special interest groups that back you. Finally, make good use of the young people who admire you and want to learn from you, in addition to all the faithful friends who are daily at your side.

4. Work to maintain the goodwill of these groups by giving them helpful advice and asking them for their counsel in return. Now is the time to call in all favors. Don't miss an opportunity to remind everyone in your debt that they should repay you with their support. For those who owe you nothing, let them know that their timely

ac numerum pervenire velis ab iis ipsis illo loco ac dignum numero putari.

5. Ii rogandi omnes sunt diligenter et ad eos adlegandum est persuadendumque iis nos semper cum optimatibus de re publica sensisse, minime popularis fuisse; si quid locuti populariter videamur, id nos eo consilio fecisse ut nobis Cn. Pompeium adiungeremus, ut eum qui plurimum posset aut amicum in nostra petitione haberemus aut certe non adversarium.

6. Praeterea adulescentis nobilis elabora ut habeas vel ut teneas, studiosos quos habes. Multum dignitatis adferent.

help will put you in their debt. And, of course, one thing that can greatly help an outsider is the backing of the nobility, particularly those who have served as consuls previously. It is essential that these men whose company you wish to join should think you worthy of them.

5. You must diligently cultivate relationships with these men of privilege. Both you and your friends should work to convince them that you have always been a traditionalist. Never let them think you are a populist. Tell them if you seem to be siding with the common people on any issue it is because you need to win the favor of Pompey, so that he can use his great influence on your behalf or at least not against you.

6. Be sure you work to get young men from noble families on your side and keep them there. They can be very helpful to

Plurimos habes; perfice ut sciant quantum in iis putes esse. Si adduxeris ut ii qui non nolunt cupiant, plurimum proderunt.

7. Ac multum etiam novitatem tuam adiuvat quod eius modi nobiles tecum petunt, ut nemo sit qui audeat dicere plus illis nobilitatem quam tibi virtutem prodesse oportere. Nam P. Galbam et L. Cassium summo loco natos quis est qui petere consulatum putet? Vides igitur amplissimis ex familiis homines, quod sine nervis sunt, tibi paris non esse.

your campaign by making you look good. You already have many supporters among this group, so make sure they know how much you appreciate them. If you can win over even more of them to your side, so much the better.

7. Another factor that can help you as an outsider is the poor quality of those men of the nobility who are competing against you. No one could reasonably say that their privileged birth makes them more qualified to be consul than your natural gifts. Who would believe that men as pathetic as Publius Galba and Lucius Cassius would run for the highest office in the land, even though they come from the best families? You can clearly see that even those from the loftiest background are not equal to you because they lack the drive.

8. At Antonius et Catilina molesti sunt. Immo homini navo, industrio, innocenti, diserto, gratioso apud eos qui res iudicant, optandi competitores ambo a pueritia sicarii, ambo libidinosi, ambo egentes. Eorum alterius bona proscripta vidimus, vocem denique audivimus iurantis se Romae iudicio aequo cum homine Graeco certare non posse, ex senatu eiectum scimus optima verorum censorum existimatione, in praetura competitorem habuimus amico Sabidio et Panthera, cum ad tabulam quos poneret non haberet; quo tamen in magistratu amicam quam domi palam haberet de machinis emit. In petitione autem consulatus caupones omnis compilare per turpissimam legationem maluit quam adesse et populo Romano supplicare.

8. But, you might say, what about the other candidates, Antonius and Catiline? Surely they are dangerous opponents? Yes, they certainly are, but not to someone like you who is energetic, hardworking, free from scandal, eloquent, and popular with those in power. You should be grateful to run against men like those two. They have both been brutes since they were boys, while even now they are notorious philanderers and spendthrifts. Consider Antonius, who had his property confiscated for debt, then declared under oath in Rome that he couldn't even compete in a fair trial against a Greek. Remember how he was expelled from the Senate after a careful examination by the censors? And don't forget that when he ran for praetor he could only muster Sabidius and Panthera to stand beside him. Then after he was elected as praetor, he disgraced

9. Alter vero, di boni! quo splendore est? Primum nobilitate eadem. Num maiore? Non. Sed virtute. Quam ob rem? Quod Antonius umbram suam metuit, hic ne leges quidem natus in patris egestate, educatus in sororis stupris, corroboratus in caede civium, cuius primus ad rem publicam aditus in equitibus Romanis occidendis fuit, nam illis quos meminimus Gallis, qui tum Titiniorum ac Nanniorum ac Tanusiorum capita demebant, Sulla unum Catilinam praefecerat, in quibus ille hominem optimum, Q. Caecilium, sororis suae virum, equitem Romanum, nullarum

himself by going down to the market and openly buying a girl to keep at home as a sex slave. Finally, who could forget that the last time he put his name up for consul he went abroad and robbed innkeepers rather than stay here in Rome and face the voters?

9. As for Catiline, by the gods, what is his claim to fame? His blood is no better than that of Antonius, but I will grant that he has more courage. He's not afraid of anything, least of all the law, while Antonius trembles at his own shadow. Catiline was born into a poor family, brought up in debauchery with his own sister, and shed his first blood killing Roman citizens and businessmen as a henchman of Sulla. You'll remember he was put in charge of the Gaulish death squads who cut off the heads of the Titinii, Nannii, and Tanusii. He even murdered his own brother-in-law, Quintus

partium, cum semper natura tum etiam aetate iam quietum, suis manibus occidit.

10. Quid ego nunc dicam petere eum consulatum, qui hominem carissimum populo Romano, M. Marium inspectante populo Romano vitibus per totam urbem ceciderit, ad bustum egerit, ibi omni cruciatu lacerarit, vivo stanti collum gladio sua dextera secuerit, cum sinistra capillum eius a vertice teneret, caput sua manu tulerit, cum inter digitos eius rivi sanguinis fluerent? qui postea cum histrionibus et cum gladiatoribus ita vixit ut alteros libidinis, alteros facinoris adiutores haberet, qui nullum in locum tam sanctum ac tam religiosum accessit in quo non, etiam si aliis culpa non esset, tamen ex sua nequitia dedecoris suspicionem relinqueret, qui ex curia Curios et Annios, ab atriis Sapalas et Carvilios,

Caecilius, a kindly old fellow and good Roman businessman who cared nothing for politics.

10. Catiline, your chief opponent in this contest, took a club and beat poor Marcus Marius, a man very popular with the Roman people. With everyone watching, the scoundrel chased Marius through the streets to a tomb where he tortured him with every cruelty. Then, still alive, he grabbed him by the hair with his left hand and decapitated him with his right and carried the head away with blood dripping between his fingers. Catiline afterward was a friend of actors—can you imagine?—and gladiators. He lived a life of debauchery with the former group and used the latter as hired thugs in all his crimes. He never missed a chance to defile a holy shrine even if his companions refused to stoop so low.

ex equestri ordine Pompilios et Vettios sibi
amicissimos comparavit, qui tantum habet
audaciae, tantum nequitiae, tantum denique
in libidine artis et efficacitatis, ut prope
in parentum gremiis praetextatos liberos
constuprarit? Quid ego nunc tibi de Africa, quid de testium dictis scribam? Nota
sunt, et ea tu saepius legito; sed tamen hoc
mihi non praetermittendum videtur quod
primum ex eo iudicio tam egens discessit
quam quidam iudices eius ante illud in eum
iudicium fuerunt, deinde tam invidiosus ut
aliud in eum iudicium cotidie flagitetur. Hic
se sic habet ut magis timeat, etiam si quierit,
quam ut contemnat si quid commoverit.

He made friends with the worst sort— Curius and Annius in the Senate, Sapala and Carvilius in the auction houses, Pompilius and Vettius among the businessmen. He was so impudent, so wicked, so skilled in his licentiousness that he molested young boys almost in the laps of their parents. Do I even need to remind you what he did in Africa? It's all recorded in the indictments, which you should take the time to review carefully, by the way. I can't forget to mention that he bribed his way through his trials so heavily that he often left the courts as poor as his judges had been before. Practically every day there is a new call to bring him to justice. He is so unpredictable that men are more afraid of him when he is doing nothing than they are when he is making trouble.

11. Quanto melior tibi fortuna petitionis data est quam nuper homini novo,
C. Coelio! Ille cum duobus hominibus ita
nobilissimis petebat ut tamen in iis omnia
pluris essent quam ipsa nobilitas, summa
ingenia, summus pudor, plurima beneficia,
summa ratio ac diligentia petendi. Ac tamen eorum alterum Coelius, cum multo
inferior esset genere, superior nulla re
paene, superavit.

12. Qua re tibi, si facies ea quae natura
et studia quibus semper usus es, largi-
untur, quae temporis tui ratio desiderat,
quae potes, quae debes, non erit difficile
certamen cum iis competitoribus, qui

11. You have a much better chance of being elected consul than another outsider, Gaius Coelius, who thirty years ago had two very different competitors than you do now. These men were of the most distinguished birth, but their other qualities were even more outstanding. They possessed the greatest integrity and intelligence, the most appealing modesty, and had accomplished many noteworthy deeds for Rome. Both managed their campaigns with consummate skill and care. Yet Coelius beat one of them to win a consulship, even though he was much inferior to them in birth and not superior to either in any notable way.

12. Therefore, if you make use of your natural gifts and apply all that you have learned in life and if you make no mistakes, it should not be difficult for you to defeat Antonius and Catiline—men who are more

nequaquam sunt tam genere insignes quam
vitiis nobiles. Quis enim reperiri potest tam
improbus civis qui velit uno suffragio duas
in rem publicam sicas destringere?

13. Quoniam quae subsidia novitatis
haberes et habere posses exposui, nunc de
magnitudine petitionis dicendum videtur.
Consulatum petis, quo honore nemo est
quin te dignum arbitretur, sed multi qui
invideant; petis enim homo ex equestri loco
summum locum civitatis atque ita summum
ut forti homini, diserto, innocenti multo
idem ille honos plus amplitudinis quam
ceteris adferat. Noli putare eos qui sunt
eo honore usi non videre, tu cum idem sis
adeptus, quid dignitatis habiturus sis. Eos
vero qui consularibus familiis nati locum
maiorum consecuti non sunt suspicor tibi,
nisi si qui admodum te amant, invidere.

distinguished by their crimes than their privileged birth. Can you find a single Roman citizen so despicable that he would in one vote unsheathe two such bloody daggers on the republic?

13. Since I have already discussed your abilities and how you can overcome the fact that you are an outsider, I want to talk about the details of how you should run your campaign. You want to be a consul and everyone agrees you have the ability to do the job, but there are many who are jealous of you. You are not part of the nobility, yet you seek the highest office in the land. Serving in this position would confer on you a tremendous distinction, especially as you are courageous, eloquent, and free from scandal, unlike so many others. Those who have held the office before know very well the glory that being consul would

Etiam novos homines praetorios existimo, nisi qui tuo beneficio vincti sunt, nolle abs te se honore superari.

14. Iam in populo quam multi invidi sint, quam consuetudine horum annorum ab hominibus novis alienati, venire tibi in mentem certo scio; esse etiam non nullos tibi iratos ex iis causis quas egisti necesse est. Iam illud tute circumspicito, quod ad Cn. Pompeii gloriam augendam tanto studio te dedisti, num quos tibi putes ob eam causam esse amicos.

15. Quam ob rem, cum et summum locum civitatis petas et videas esse studia

bestow on you. Those whose ancestors were consuls but who have not yet gained it for themselves are going to be envious, unless they are already very good friends of yours. As for the outsiders who have made it to the office of praetor before you but not held the consulship, they are going to be bitterly jealous, save for those who are greatly in your debt.

14. I know very well that there are many others who despise you. With the turmoil of the last few years, plenty of voters don't want to risk electing an outsider. There are also those who are angry at you regarding the clients you defended in court. And take a close look at those supposed friends of yours who might be secretly furious that you have so zealously supported Pompey.

15. To speak bluntly, since you are seeking the most important position in

quae adversentur, adhibeas necesse est omnem rationem et curam et laborem et diligentiam.

16. Et petitio magistratus divisa est in duarum rationum diligentiam, quarum altera in amicorum studiis, altera in populari voluntate ponenda est. Amicorum studia beneficiis et officiis et vetustate et facilitate ac iucunditate naturae parta esse oportet. Sed hoc nomen amicorum in petitione latius patet quam in cetera vita. Quisquis est enim qui ostendat aliquid in te voluntatis, qui colat, qui domum ventitet, is in amicorum numero est habendus. Sed tamen, qui sunt amici ex causa iustiore cognationis aut adfinitatis aut sodalitatis aut alicuius necessitudinis, iis carum et iucundum esse maxime prodest.

Rome and since you have so many potential enemies, you can't afford to make any mistakes. You must conduct a flawless campaign with the greatest thoughtfulness, industry, and care.

16. Running for office can be divided into two kinds of activity: securing the support of your friends and winning over the general public. You gain the goodwill of friends through kindness, favors, old connections, availability, and natural charm. But in an election you need to think of friendship in broader terms than in everyday life. For a candidate, a friend is anyone who shows you goodwill or seeks out your company. But don't neglect those who are your friends in the traditional sense through family ties or social connection. These you must continue to carefully cultivate.

17. Deinde, ut quisque est intimus ac maxime domesticus, ut is amet et quam amplissimum esse te cupiat, valde elaborandum est, tum ut tribules, ut vicini, ut clientes, ut denique liberti, postremo etiam servi tui; nam fere omnis sermo ad forensem famam a domesticis emanat auctoribus.

18. Denique sunt instituendi cuiusque generis amici, ad speciem homines inlustres honore ac nomine, qui etiam si suffragandi studia non navant, tamen adferunt petitori aliquid dignitatis; ad ius obtinendum magistratus, ex quibus maxime consules, deinde tribuni plebi, ad conficiendas centurias homines excellenti gratia. Qui abs te tribum aut centuriam aut aliquod beneficium aut habeant aut sperent, eos rursus magno opere et compara et confirma. Nam per hos annos homines ambitiosi vehementer omni

17. Do not overlook your family and those closely connected with you. Make sure they all are behind you and want you to succeed. This includes your tribe, your neighbors, your clients, your former slaves, and even your servants. For almost every destructive rumor that makes its way to the public begins among family and friends.

18. You should work with diligence to secure supporters from a wide variety of backgrounds. Most important among these are men of distinguished reputations, for even if they don't actively back you they will confer dignity on you by mere association. Work to win over former magistrates, including those who have been consuls but also tribunes of the people, for this makes you look worthy of holding high office. Make friends with any man who holds great influence among the centuries and tribes,

studio atque opera elaborant, ut possint a
tribulibus suis ea quae petierint impetrare.
Hos tu homines, quibuscumque poteris
rationibus, ut ex animo atque ex illa summa
voluntate tui studiosi sint elaborato.

19. Quod si satis grati homines essent,
haec tibi omnia parata esse debebant, sic
uti parata esse confido. Nam hoc biennio
quattuor sodalitates hominum ad ambitionem gratiosissimorum tibi obligasti, C.
Fundani, Q. Galli, C. Corneli, C. Orcivi.
Horum in causis ad te deferendis quid tibi
eorum sodales receperint et confirmarint
scio, nam interfui. Qua re hoc tibi facien-
dum est, hoc tempore ut ab his quod debent exigas saepe commonendo, rogando,
confirmando, curando ut intelligant nullum se umquam aliud tempus habituros
referendae gratiae. Profecto homines et
spe reliquorum tuorum officiorum et iam

then work to keep them on your side. In recent years ambitious men have labored to gain influence over their fellow tribesmen, so do whatever it takes to make them support you sincerely and enthusiastically.

19. If men are sufficiently grateful to you, as I'm sure they are, everything will fall into place. Over the last two years you have been diligent in gaining the support of four key organizations, those run by Gaius Fundanius, Quintus Gallius, Gaius Cornelius, and Gaius Orcivius—all men of the greatest importance for the success of your campaign. I know about the agreements these four made with you to represent their interests, since I was there at the meetings. So now is time to press home their obligations to you through frequent requests, assurances, encouragement, and admonition. Again, tell them this is the occasion to pay

recentibus beneficiis ad studium navandum excitabuntur.

20. Et omnino quoniam eo genere amicitiarum petitio tua maxime munita est, quod ex causarum defensionibus adeptus es, fac ut plane iis omnibus quos devinctos tenes descriptum ac dispositum suum cuique munus sit; et quem ad modum nemini illorum molestus ulla in re umquam fuisti, sic cura ut intelligant omnia te quae ab illis tibi deberi putaris ad hoc tempus reservasse.

21. Sed, quoniam tribus rebus homines maxime ad benevolentiam atque haec suffragandi studia ducuntur, beneficio, spe, adiunctione animi ac voluntate, animadvertendum est quem ad modum cuique horum generi sit inserviendum.

Minimis beneficiis homines adducuntur ut satis causae putent esse ad studium suffragationis, nedum ii quibus saluti fuisti,

their political debts to you if they want you to look favorably on them in the future.

20. Remember also those men who owe you favors because you defended their interests successfully in court. Make it clear to each one under obligation to you exactly what you expect from him. Remind them that you have never asked anything of them before, but now is the time to make good on what they owe you.

21. There are three things that will guarantee votes in an election: favors, hope, and personal attachment. You must work to give these incentives to the right people.

You can win uncommitted voters to your side by doing them even small favors. So much more so all those you have greatly

quos tu habes plurimos, non intellegant, si hoc tuo tempore tibi non satis fecerint, se probatos nemini umquam fore. Quod cum ita sit, tamen rogandi sunt atque etiam in hanc opinionem adducendi ut qui adhuc nobis obligati fuerint iis vicissim nos obligari posse videamur.

22. Qui autem spe tenentur, quod genus hominum multo etiam est diligentius atque officiosius, iis fac ut propositum ac paratum auxilium tuum esse videatur, denique ut spectatorem te officiorum esse intellegant diligentem, ut videre te plane atque animadvertere quantum a quoque proficiscatur appareat.

23. Tertium illud genus est studiorum voluntarium, quod agendis gratiis, accommodandis sermonibus ad eas rationes, propter quas quisque studiosus tui esse videbitur, significanda erga illos pari

helped, who must be made to understand that if they don't support you now they will lose all public respect. But do go to them in person and let them know that if they back you in this election you will be in their debt.

22. As for those who you have inspired with hope—a zealous and devoted group— you must make them to believe that you will always be there to help them. Let them know that you are grateful for their loyalty and that you are keenly aware of and appreciate what each of them is doing for you.

23. The third class of supporters are those who show goodwill because of a personal attachment they believe they have made with you. Encourage this by adapting your message to fit the particular

voluntate, adducenda amicitia in spem familiaritatis et consuetudinis confirmari oportebit.

Atque in iis omnibus generibus iudicato et perpendito, quantum quisque possit, ut scias et quem ad modum cuique inservias et quid a quoque exspectes ac postules.

24. Sunt enim quidam homines in suis vicinitatibus et municipiis gratiosi, sunt diligentes et copiosi, qui etiam si antea non studuerunt huic gratiae, tamen ex tempore elaborare eius causa cui debent aut volunt, facile possunt. His hominum generibus sic inserviendum est ut ipsi intelligant te videre quid a quoque exspectes, sentire quid accipias, meminisse quid acceperis. Sunt autem alii, qui aut nihil possunt aut etiam odio sunt tribulibus suis nec habent

circumstances of each and showing abundant goodwill to them in return. Show them that the more they work for your election the closer your bond to them will be.

For each of these three groups of supporters, decide how they can help you in your campaign and give attention to each accordingly, reckoning as well how much you can demand from them.

24. There are certain key men in every neighborhood and town who exercise power. These are diligent and wealthy people who, in spite of not backing you previously, can be persuaded to support you if they feel indebted to you or see you as useful to them. As you cultivate relationships with these men, make sure they realize that you know what you can expect from them, that you recognize what they have done for you, and that you will

tantum animi ac facultatis ut enitantur ex tempore. Hos ut internoscas, elaborato, ne spe in aliquo maiore posita praesidi parum comparetur.

25. Et quamquam partis ac fundatis amicitiis fretum ac munitum esse oportet, tamen in ipsa petitione amicitiae permultae ac perutiles comparantur; nam in ceteris molestiis habet hoc tamen petitio commodi, potes honeste, quod in cetera vita non queas, quoscumque velis adiungere ad amicitiam, quibuscum si alio tempore agas, absurde facere videare, in petitione autem nisi id agas et cum multis et diligenter, nullus petitor esse videare.

remember their work for you. But be sure to distinguish these men from those who seem important but have no real power and in fact are often unpopular in their group. Recognizing the difference between the useful and useless men in any organization will save you from investing your time and resources with people who will be of little help to you.

25. Although the friendships that you have already established and confirmed should be a great help and strengthen your chances of winning the consulship, the friendships you make while campaigning can also be very useful. Running for office, as wearisome as it is, has the advantage of allowing you to meet and get to know many different types of people you wouldn't normally associate with in your daily life. This is perfectly respectable during a

26. Ego autem tibi hoc confirmo, esse neminem, nisi aliqua necessitudine competitorum alicui tuorum sit adiunctus, a quo non facile si contenderis impetrare possis ut suo beneficio promereatur se ut ames et sibi ut debeas, modo ut intelligat te magni aestimare ex animo agere, bene se ponere, fore ex eo non brevem et suffragatoriam sed firmam et perpetuam amicitiam.

27. Nemo erit, mihi crede, in quo modo aliquid sit, qui hoc tempus sibi oblatum amicitiae tecum constituendae praetermittat, praesertim cum tibi hoc casus adferat ut ii tecum petant quorum amicitia aut

campaign—in fact you would be thought a fool if you didn't take advantage of it—so that you can eagerly and unashamedly cultivate friendships with people no decent person would talk to.

26. I assure you that there is nobody, except perhaps ardent supporters of your opponents, who cannot be won over to your side with hard work and proper favors. But this will only work if a man sees that you value his support, that you are sincere, that you can do something for him, and that the relationship will extend beyond election day.

27. Believe me, no one with any brains at all will pass on the chance to strike up a friendship with you, especially as your competitors are not the sort anyone would want as friends. Your opponents could not

contemnenda aut fugienda sit, et qui hoc quod ego te hortor non modo adsequi sed ne incipere quidem possint.

28. Nam qui incipiat Antonius homines adiungere atque invitare ad amicitiam quos per se suo nomine appellare non possit? Mihi quidem nihil stultius videtur quam existimare esse eum studiosum tui quem non noris. Eximiam quandam gloriam et dignitatem ac rerum gestarum magnitudinem esse oportet in eo quem homines ignoti nullis suffragantibus honore afficiant; ut quidem homo nequam, iners, sine officio, sine ingenio, cum infamia, nullis amicis hominem plurimorum studio atque omnium bona existimatione munitum praecurrat, sine magna culpa negligentiae fieri non potest.

29. Quam ob rem omnis centurias multis et variis amicitiis cura ut confirmatas

begin to heed the advice I am giving you, let alone follow it through.

28. Look at Antonius—how can the man establish friendships when he can't even remember anyone's name? Can there be anything sillier than for a candidate to think a person he doesn't know will support him? It would take miraculous ability, renown, and accomplishments to win over voters without taking the time to talk to them. A lazy scoundrel, unwilling to work for supporters, lacking intelligence, having a poor reputation, and possessing no friends cannot possibly beat a man backed by many and admired by all unless something goes horribly wrong.

29. Therefore work to obtain the support of all the voters by making friends of

habeas. Et primum, id quod ante oculos est, senatores equitesque Romanos, ceterorum ordinum navos homines et gratiosos complectere. Multi homines urbani industrii, multi libertini in foro gratiosi navique versantur. Quos per te, quos per communis amicos poteris, summa cura ut cupidi tui sint elaborato, appetito, adlegato, summo beneficio te adfici ostendito.

30. Deinde habeto rationem urbis totius, collegiorum omnium, pagorum, vicinitatum. Ex his principes ad amicitiam tuam si adiunxeris, per eos reliquam multitudinem facile tenebis. Postea totam Italiam fac ut in animo ac memoria tributim descriptam comprehensamque habeas, ne quod municipium, coloniam, praefecturam, locum denique Italiae ne quem esse patiare in quo non habeas firmamenti quod satis esse possit.

various sorts. This should include senators, of course, as well as Roman businessmen and important men of all classes. There are plenty of influential people in this city in addition to numerous freed slaves who frequent the Forum. As much as you can, whether on your own or through your friends, work to bring them to your cause. Talk to them, send your allies, do everything possible to show them that they matter to you.

30. After this turn your attention to the special interest groups, the neighborhood organizations, and the outlying districts. If you make the leading men from each of these your friends, the rest will follow along. Then turn your efforts and thoughts to the towns of Italy so that you know which tribe each belongs to. Make sure you have a foothold in every colony, village, and farm in Italy.

31. Perquiras et investiges homines ex omni regione, eos cognoscas, appetas, confirmes, cures ut in suis vicinitatibus tibi petant et tua causa quasi candidati sint. Volent te amicum, si suam a te amicitiam expeti videbunt. Id ut intelligant oratione ea quae ad eam rationem pertinet habenda consequere. Homines municipales ac rusticani, si nobis nomine noti sunt, in amicitia esse se arbitrantur; si vero etiam praesidi se aliquid sibi constituere putant, non amittunt occasionem promerendi. Hos ceteri et maxime tui competitores ne norunt quidem, tu et nosti et facile cognosces, sine quo amicitia esse non potest.

32. Neque id tamen satis est, tametsi magnum est, sed sequitur spes utilitatis

31. Seek out men everywhere who will represent you as if they themselves where running for office. Visit them, talk to them, get to know them. Strengthen their loyalty to you in whatever way works best, using the language they understand. They will want to be your friends if they see that you want to be theirs. Small-town men and country folk will want to be your friends if you take the trouble to learn their names—but they are not fools. They will only support you if they believe they have something to gain. If so, they will miss no chance to help you. Others, especially your competitors, won't trouble themselves to develop friendships with these sorts of people, so if you take the time, they can be all the more valuable to you as friends and allies.

32. But with any class of people, it isn't enough that you merely call them by name

atque amicitiae, ne nomenclator solum sed amicus etiam bonus esse videare. Ita cum et hos ipsos, propter suam ambitionem qui apud tribulis suos plurimum gratia possunt, studiosos in centuriis habebis et ceteros qui apud aliquam partem tribulium propter municipi aut vicinitatis aut conlegi rationem valent cupidos tui constitueris, in optima spe esse debebis.

33. Iam equitum centuriae multo facilius mihi diligentia posse teneri videntur. Primum cognosce equites, pauci enim sunt, deinde appete, multo enim facilius illa adulescentulorum ad amicitiam aetas adiungitur, deinde habes tecum ex iuventute optimum quemque et studiosissimum humanitatis; tum autem, quod equester ordo tuus est, sequuntur illi auctoritatem ordinis, si abs te adhibetur ea diligentia

and develop a superficial friendship. You must actually be their friend. When they believe you are, the leaders of any organization will rally their members to work hard for you since they know that backing you will naturally benefit them as well. Thus when all your supporters among the towns, neighborhoods, tribes, and various groups are working together on your behalf, you should feel very hopeful indeed.

33. You should pay special attention to the centuries that represent the businessmen and moderately wealthy citizens. Get to know the leading members of these groups, which shouldn't be difficult as they are not great in number. Most of them are young men, so they should be easier to win over than those already set in their ways. Do this and you will have the best and the brightest of Rome on your side. This effort

ut non ordinis solum voluntate sed etiam singulorum amicitiis eas centurias confirmatas habeas. Iam studia adulescentulorum in suffragando, in obeundo, in nuntiando, in adsectando mirifice et magna et honesta sunt.

34. Et, quoniam adsectationis mentio facta est, id quoque curandum est ut cotidiana cuiusque generis et ordinis et aetatis utare. Nam ex ea ipsa copia coniectura fieri poterit quantum sis in ipso campo virium ac facultatis habiturus. Huius autem rei tres partes sunt, una salutatorum, altera deductorum, tertia adsectatorum.

35. In salutatoribus, qui magis vulgares sunt et hac consuetudine quae nunc

will be greatly aided by the fact that you are one of them, as long as you work to secure this voting block by making friends with their leaders and serving the interests of the group as a whole. It will help your campaign tremendously to have the enthusiasm and energy of young people on your side to canvass voters, gain supporters, spread news, and make you look good.

34. Since I have touched on the subject of followers, let me also say that you must have a wide variety of people around you on a daily basis. Voters will judge you on what sort of crowd you draw both in quality and numbers. The three types of followers are those who greet you at home, those who escort you down to the Forum, and those who accompany you wherever you go.

35. As for the first type, they are the least reliable since many will make

est plures veniunt, hoc efficiendum est ut
hoc ipsum minimum officium eorum tibi
gratissimum esse videatur. Qui domum
tuam venient, significato te animadvertere;
eorum amicis qui illis renuntient ostendito, saepe ipsis dicito. Sic homines saepe,
cum obeunt pluris competitores et vident
unum esse aliquem qui haec officia maxime
animadvertat, ei se dedunt, deserunt ceteros, minutatim ex communibus proprii,
ex fucosis firmi suffragatores evadunt.
Iam illud teneto diligenter, si eum qui tibi
promiserit audieris fucum, ut dicitur, facere
aut senseris, ut te id audisse aut scire dis-
simules, si qui tibi se purgare volet quod
suspectum esse se arbitretur, adfirmes te
de illius voluntate numquam dubitasse nec
debere dubitare. Is enim qui se non putat
satis facere amicus esse nullo modo potest.
Scire autem oportet quo quisque animo sit,

domestic calls on more than one candidate. Nonetheless, make it clear to them that you are pleased to have them drop by. Mention your gratitude for their visit whenever you see them and tell their friends that you noticed their presence as well, for the friends will repeat your words to them. Even if they visit several candidates, you can win them to your side as solid supporters by taking special notice of them. If you hear or suspect that one of your callers is not as firm in his support for you as he might appear, pretend this isn't the case. If he tries to explain that the charges are untrue, assure him that you have never doubted his loyalty and certainly won't in the future. By making him believe you trust him as a friend, you increase the chances that he really will be. Still, don't be foolish

ut quantum cuique confidas constituere possis.

36. Iam deductorum officium quo maius est quam salutatorum, hoc gratius tibi esse significato atque ostendito et, quod eius fieri poterit, certis temporibus descendito. Magnam adfert opinionem, magnam dignitatem cotidiana in deducendo frequentia.

37. Tertia est ex hoc genere adsidua adsectatorum copia. In ea quos voluntarios habebis, curato ut intellegant te sibi in perpetuum summo beneficio obligari; qui autem tibi debent, ab iis plane hoc munus exigito, qui per aetatem ac negotium poterunt, ipsi tecum ut adsidui sint, qui ipsi sectari non poterunt, suos necessarios in hoc munere constituant. Valde ego te volo et ad rem pertinere arbitror semper cum multitudine esse.

and accept every profession of goodwill you hear.

36. For those who accompany you to the Forum, let them know that you appreciate this even more than their coming to your house each morning. Try to go there at the same time each day so that you can have a large crowd following you. This will impress everyone greatly.

37. For the rest who accompany you throughout the day, make sure those who come of their own free will know how grateful you are for their company. For those who follow you because of obligation, insist that they come every day unless they are too old or are engaged in important business. If they can't make it, have them send a relative to take their place. It is vital that you have a crowd of devoted followers with you at all times.

38. Praeterea magnam adferet laudem et summam dignitatem, si ii tecum erunt qui a te defensi et qui per te servati ac iudiciis liberati sunt. Haec tu plane ab his postulato ut quoniam nulla impensa per te alii rem, alii honorem, alii salutem ac fortunas omnis obtinuerint, nec aliud ullum tempus futurum sit ubi tibi referre gratiam possint, hoc te officio remunerentur.

39. Et quoniam in amicorum studiis haec omnis oratio versatur, qui locus in hoc genere cavendus sit praetermittendum non videtur. Fraudis atque insidiarum et perfidiae plena sunt omnia. Non est huius temporis perpetua illa de hoc genere disputatio, quibus rebus benevolus et simulator diiudicari possit; tantum est huius temporis admonere. Summa tua virtus eosdem homines et simulare tibi se esse amicos et invidere

38. Part of this group under obligation to you are those you have successfully defended in lawsuits. These men owe to you the preservation of their property, reputations, and in some cases their lives, so don't be timid about demanding they stand beside you. There won't be another opportunity like this, so they should certainly repay their debt to you with their presence.

39. Since I have been writing so much on the subject of friendship, I think now is the time to sound a note of caution. Politics is full of deceit, treachery, and betrayal. I'm not going to begin a long-winded discussion of how to separate true friends from false, but I do want to give you some simple advice. Your good nature has in the past led some men to feign friendship while they were in fact jealous of you, so remember

coegit. Quam ob rem Epicharmeion illud teneto, nervos atque artus esse sapientiae non temere credere.

40. Et cum tuorum amicorum studia constitueris, tum etiam obtrectatorum atque adversariorum rationes et genera cognoscito. Haec tria sunt, unum quos laesisti, alterum qui sine causa non amant, tertium qui competitorum valde amici sunt. Quos laesisti, cum contra eos pro amico diceres, iis te plane purgato, necessitudines commemorato, in spem adducito te in eorum rebus, si se in amicitiam tuam contulerint, pari studio atque officio futurum. Qui sine causa non amant, eos aut beneficio aut spe aut significando tuo erga illos studio dato operam ut de illa animi pravitate deducas. Quorum voluntas erit abs te propter competitorum amicitias alienior, iis quoque eadem inservito ratione qua superioribus et,

the wise words of Epicharmus: "Don't trust people too easily."

40. Once you have figured out who your true friends are, give some thought to your enemies as well. There are three kinds of people who will stand against you: those you have harmed, those who dislike you for no good reason, and those who are close friends of your opponents. For those you have harmed by standing up for a friend against them, be gracious and apologetic, reminding them you were only defending someone you had strong ties to and that you would do the same for them if they were your friend. For those who don't like you without good cause, try to win them over by being kind to them or doing them a favor or by showing concern for them. As for the last group who are

si probare poteris, te in eos ipsos competitores tuos benevolo esse animo ostendito.

41. Quoniam de amicitiis constituendis
satis dictum est, dicendum est de illa altera
parte petitionis quae in populari ratione
versatur. Ea desiderat nomenclationem,
blanditiam, adsiduitatem, benignitatem,
rumorem, spem in re publica.

42. Primum quod facis, ut homines
noris, significa ut appareat, et auge ut cotidie melius fiat. Nihil mihi tam populare
neque tam gratum videtur.

Deinde id quod natura non habes induc
in animum ita simulandum esse ut natura
facere videare. Nam comitas tibi non deest,
ea quae bono ac suavi homine digna est,
sed opus est magno opere blanditia, quae
etiamsi vitiosa est et turpis in cetera vita,

friends of your rivals, you can use the same techniques, proving your benevolence even to those who are your enemies.

41. I have said enough about developing political friendships, so now I would like to focus on impressing the voters at large. This is done by knowing who people are, being personable and generous, promoting yourself, being available, and never giving up.

42. First, nothing impresses an average voter more than having a candidate remember him, so work every day to recall names and faces.

Now, my brother, you have many wonderful qualities, but those you lack you must acquire and it must appear as if you were born with them. You have excellent manners and are always courteous, but you can be rather stiff at times. You desperately

tamen in petitione est necessaria. Etenim cum deteriorem aliquem adsentando facit, tum improba est, cum amiciorem, non tam vituperanda, petitori vero necessaria est, cuius frons et vultus et sermo ad eorum quoscumque convenerit sensum et voluntatem commutandus et accommodandus est.

43. Iam adsiduitatis nullum est praeceptum, verbum ipsum docet quae res sit. Prodest quidem vehementer nusquam discedere, sed tamen hic fructus est adsiduitatis, non solum esse Romae atque in foro sed adsidue petere, saepe eosdem appellare, non committere ut quisquam possit dicere, quod eius consequi possis, si abs te non sit rogatum et valde ac diligenter rogatum.

44. Benignitas autem late patet. Est in re familiari, quae quamquam ad multitudinem

need to learn the art of flattery — a disgraceful thing in normal life but essential when you are running for office. If you use flattery to corrupt a man there is no excuse for it, but if you apply ingratiation as a way to make political friends, it is acceptable. For a candidate must be a chameleon, adapting to each person he meets, changing his expression and speech as necessary.

43. Don't leave Rome! Being assiduous means to stay put and that is what you must do. There is no time for vacations during a campaign. Be present in the city and in the Forum, speaking constantly with voters, then talking with them again the next day and the next. Never let anyone be able to say that he lacked your earnest and repeated attention during the campaign.

44. Generosity is also a requirement of a candidate, even if it doesn't affect most

pervenire non potest, tamen ab amicis si laudatur, multitudini grata est; est in conviviis, quae fac et abs te et ab amicis tuis concelebrentur et passim et tributim; est etiam in opera, quam pervulga et communica, curaque ut aditus ad te diurni nocturnique pateant, neque solum foribus aedium tuarum sed etiam vultu ac fronte, quae est animi ianua; quae si significat voluntatem abditam esse ac retrusam, parvi refert patere ostium. Homines enim non modo promitti sibi, praesertim quod a candidato petant, sed etiam large atque honorifice promitti volunt.

45. Qua re hoc quidem facile praeceptum est, ut quod facturus sis id significes te studiose ac libenter esse facturum; illud difficilius et magis ad tempus quam

voters directly. People like to hear that you are good to your friends at events such as banquets, so make sure that you and your allies celebrate these frequently for the leaders of each tribe. Another way to show you are generous is to be available day and night to those who need you. Keep the doors of your house open, of course, but also open your face and expression, for these are the window to the soul. If you look closed and distracted when people talk with you, it won't matter that your front gates are never locked. People not only want commitments from a candidate but they want them delivered in an engaged and generous manner.

45. Thus whatever you do you must do freely and with enthusiasm. But sometimes you must do something more difficult, especially for a man of your good nature, and

ad naturam accommodatum tuam, quod
facere non possis, ut id aut iucunde neges
aut etiam non neges quorum alterum est
tamen boni viri, alterum boni petitoris.
Nam cum id petitur, quod honeste aut sine
detrimento nostro promittere non pos-
sumus, quo modo si qui roget ut contra
amicum aliquem causam recipiamus, belle
negandum est, ut ostendas necessitudinem,
demonstres quam moleste feras, aliis te
rebus exsarturum esse persuadeas.

46. Audivi hoc dicere quendam de
quibusdam oratoribus, ad quos causam
suam detulisset, gratiorem sibi orationem
eius fuisse qui negasset quam illius qui
recepisset. Sic homines fronte et oratione
magis quam ipso beneficio reque capiuntur.
Verum hoc probabile est, illud alterum
subdurum tibi homini Platonico suadere,

that is to say no graciously when someone asks you to do something for him. The other option is to always say yes—a path often taken by political candidates. But when someone asks you to do something impossible, such as taking sides against a friend, you must, of course, refuse as a matter of honor, explaining your commitment to your friend, expressing your regret at turning down the request, and promising that you will make it up to him in other ways.

46. But saying no is only for such extreme cases. I once heard about a man who asked several lawyers to take his case, but was more pleased by the kind words of the one who refused him than those who agreed to represent him. This shows that people are moved more by appearances than reality, though I realize this course is

sed tamen tempori consulam. Quibus enim te propter aliquod officium necessitudinis adfuturum negaris, tamen ii possunt abs te placati aequique discedere; quibus autem idcirco negaris, quod te impeditum esse dixeris aut amicorum hominum negotiis aut gravioribus causis aut ante susceptis, inimici discedunt omnesque hoc animo sunt ut sibi te mentiri malint quam negare.

47. C. Cotta, in ambitione artifex, dicere solebat se operam suam, quod non contra officium rogaretur, polliceri solere omnibus, impertire iis apud quos optime poni arbitraretur; ideo se nemini negare, quod saepe accideret causa cur is cui pollicitus esset non uteretur, saepe ut ipse magis esset vacuus quam putasset; neque posse eius domum compleri qui tantum

difficult to for someone like you who is a follower of the philosopher Plato. Still, I am telling you what you need to hear as a candidate for public office. If you refuse a man by making up some tale about a personal commitment to a friend, he can walk away without being angry at you. But if you say you're just too busy or have more important things to do, he will hate you. People would prefer you give them a gracious lie than an outright refusal.

47. Remember Cotta, that master of campaigning, who said that he would promise everything to anyone, unless some clear obligation prevented him, but only lived up to those promises that benefited him. He seldom refused anyone, for he said that often a person he made a promise to would end up not needing him or that he himself would have more time available

modo reciperet quantum videret se obire posse; casu fieri ut agantur ea quae non putaris, illa, quae credideris in manibus esse ut aliqua de causa non agantur; deinde esse extremum ut irascatur is cui mendacium dixeris.

48. Id, si promittas, et incertum est et in diem et in paucioribus; sin autem neges, et certe abalienes et statim et plures. Plures enim multo sunt qui rogant ut uti liceat opera alterius quam qui utuntur. Qua re satius est ex his aliquos aliquando in foro tibi irasci quam omnis continuo domi, praesertim cum multo magis irascantur iis qui negent, quam ei quem videant ea ex causa impeditum, ut facere quod promisit cupiat si ullo modo possit.

than he thought he would to help. After all, if a politician made only promises he was sure he could keep, he wouldn't have many friends. Events are always happening that you didn't expect or not happening that you did expect. Broken promises are often lost in a cloud of changing circumstances so that anger against you will be minimal.

48. If you break a promise, the outcome is uncertain and the number of people affected is small. But if you refuse to make a promise, the result is certain and produces immediate anger in a larger number of voters. Most of those who ask for your help will never actually need it. Thus it is better to have a few people in the Forum disappointed when you let them down than have a mob outside your home when you refuse to promise them what they want. People

49. Ac ne videar aberrasse a distributione mea, qui haec in hac populari parte
petitionis disputem, hoc sequor, haec
omnia non tam ad amicorum studia quam
ad popularem famam pertinere, et si inest
aliquid ex illo genere, benigne respondere,
studiose inservire negotiis ac periculis
amicorum, tamen hoc loco ea dico, quibus
multitudinem capere possis, ut de nocte
domus compleatur, ut multi spe tui praesi-
dii teneantur, ut amiciores abs te discedant
quam accesserint, ut quam plurimorum
aures optimo sermone compleantur.

will by nature be much angrier with a man who has turned them down outright than with someone who has backed out of his obligation claiming that he would love to help them if only he could.

49. Don't think I've strayed from my topic in discussing promises under the heading of winning over the masses since it concerns your reputation among the broader electorate just as much as it does the support of friends. The latter group requires kindly responses and zealous service from you when it is in need, but now I am talking about the general public. You need to win these voters to your side so that you can fill your house with supporters every morning, hold them to you by promises of your protection, and send them away more enthusiastic about your cause than when

50. Sequitur enim ut de rumore dicendum sit, cui maxime serviendum est. Sed quae dicta sunt omni superiore oratione, eadem ad rumorem concelebrandum valent, dicendi laus, studia publicanorum et equestris ordinis, hominum nobilium voluntas, adolescentulorum frequentia, eorum qui abs te defensi sunt adsiduitas, ex municipiis multitudo eorum, quos tua causa venisse appareat, bene te ut homines nosse, comiter appellare, adsidue ac diligenter petere, benignum ac liberalem esse et loquantur et existiment, domus ut multa nocte compleatur, omnium generum frequentia adsit, satis fiat oratione omnibus, re operaque multis; perficiatur id quod fieri potest labore et arte ac diligentia, non ut ad populum ab his

they came so that more and more people hear good things about you.

50. You must always think about publicity. I've been talking about this throughout my whole letter, but it is vital that you use all of your assets to spread the word about your campaign to the widest possible audience. Your ability as a public speaker is key, as is the support of the business community and those who carry out public contracts. Need I mention again the backing of the nobility, the brightest young people, those you have defended in court, and the leaders of the Italian towns? Having these groups behind you will cause the populace to think you are well connected, have many important friends, are a hardworking candidate, and that you are a gracious and generous person. This will

omnibus fama perveniat sed ut in his studiis populus ipse versetur.

51. Iam urbanam illam multitudinem et eorum studia qui contiones tenent adeptus es in Pompeio ornando, Manili causa recipienda, Cornelio defendendo: excitanda nobis sunt, quae adhuc habuit nemo quin idem splendidorum hominum voluntates haberet. Efficiendum etiam illud est ut sciant omnes Cn. Pompei summam esse erga te voluntatem et vehementer ad illius rationes te id assequi quod petis pertinere.

52. Postremo tota petitio cura ut pompae plena sit, ut inlustris, ut splendida, ut

fill your house with supporters of every kind before sunrise. To these you should say whatever is necessary to please them as you labor endlessly to win the votes of all. Work hard to do this and you will personally win over many of the common people rather than just have them hear good things about you from friends.

51. You already have the support of the Roman crowd and those who influence them by your praise of Pompey and defense of his men, Manilius and Cornelius. You must now do what no one has done before and add to your popular base the support of the nobility. But never stop reminding the common people that you have won the goodwill of their hero Pompey and that for you to be consul would please him greatly.

52. Finally, as regards the Roman masses, be sure to put on a good show.

popularis sit, ut habeat summam speciem ac dignitatem, ut etiam si quae possit ne competitoribus tuis existat aut sceleris aut libidinis aut largitionis accommodata ad eorum mores infamia.

53. Atque etiam in hac petitione maxime videndum est ut spes rei publicae bona de te sit et honesta opinio; nec tamen in petendo res publica capessenda est neque in senatu neque in contione, sed haec tibi sunt retinenda ut senatus te existimet ex eo quod ita vixeris defensorem auctoritatis suae fore, equites et viri boni ac locupletes ex vita acta te studiosum oti ac rerum tranquillarum, multitudo ex eo quod dumtaxat oratione in contionibus ac iudicio popularis fuisti, te a suis commodis non alienum futurum.

Dignified, yes, but full of the color and spectacle that appeals so much to crowds. It also wouldn't hurt to remind them of what scoundrels your opponents are and to smear these men at every opportunity with the crimes, sexual scandals, and corruption they have brought on themselves.

53. The most important part of your campaign is to bring hope to people and a feeling of goodwill toward you. On the other hand, you should not make specific pledges either to the Senate or the people. Stick to vague generalities. Tell the Senate you will maintain its traditional power and privileges. Let the business community and wealthy citizens know that you are for stability and peace. Assure the common people that you have always been on their side, both in your speeches and in your defense of their interests in court.

54. Haec veniebant mihi in mentem de duabus illis commentationibus matutinis, quod tibi cotidie ad Forum descendenti meditandum esse dixeram: "Novus sum, consulatum peto." Tertium restat: "Roma est," civitas ex nationum conventu constituta, in qua multae insidiae, multa fallacia, multa in omni genere vitia versantur, multorum adrogantia, multorum contumacia, multorum malevolentia, multorum superbia, multorum odium ac molestia perferenda est. Video esse magni consili atque artis in tot hominum cuiusque modi vitiis tantisque versantem vitare offensionem, vitare fabulam, vitare insidias, esse unum hominem accommodatum ad tantam morum ac sermonum ac voluntatum varietatem.

55. Qua re etiam atque etiam perge tenere istam viam quam institisti, excelle dicendo. Hoc et tenentur Romae et

54. All these things have occurred to me regarding the first two of the morning meditations I suggested as you go down to the Forum: "I am an outsider. I want to be a consul." Now let me turn briefly to the third: "This is Rome." Our city is a cesspool of humanity, a place of deceit, plots, and vice of every imaginable kind. Anywhere you turn you will see arrogance, stubbornness, malevolence, pride, and hatred. Amid such a swirl of evil, it takes a remarkable man with sound judgment and great skill to avoid stumbling, gossip, and betrayal. How many men could maintain their integrity while adapting themselves to various ways of behaving, speaking, and feeling?

55. In such a chaotic world, you must stick to the path you have chosen. It is your unmatched skill as a speaker that

adliciuntur et ab impediendo ac laedendo repelluntur. Et quoniam in hoc vel maxime est vitiosa civitas, quod largitione interposita virtutis ac dignitatis oblivisci solet, in hoc fac ut te bene noris, id est ut intelligas eum esse te qui iudicii ac periculi metum maximum competitoribus adferre possis.

Fac se ut abs te custodiri atque observari sciant; cum diligentiam tuam, cum auctoritatem vimque dicendi tum profecto equestris ordinis erga te studium pertimescent.

56. Atque haec ita volo te illis proponere non ut videare accusationem iam meditari, sed ut hoc terrore facilius hoc ipsum quod agis consequare. Et plane sic contende omnibus nervis ac facultatibus ut adipiscamur quod petimus. Video nulla esse comitia tam inquinata largitione quibus non gratis aliquae centuriae renuntient suos magno opere necessarios.

draws the Roman people to you and keeps them on your side. It may well be that your opponents will try to use bribery to win your supporters from you, for this can often work. But let them know you will be watching their actions most carefully and you will haul them into court. They will be afraid of your attention and oratory, as well as the influence your have with the business community.

56. You don't have to actually bring your opponents to trial on corruption charges, just let them know you are willing to do so. Fear works even better than actual litigation. And don't be discouraged by all this talk of bribery. I am certain that even in the most corrupt elections that there are plenty of voters who support the candidates they believe in without money changing hands.

57. Qua re si advigilamus pro rei digni-
tate et si nostros ad summum studium be-
nevolos excitamus et si hominibus studiosis
gratiosisque nostri suum cuique munus
discribimus et si competitoribus iudicium
proponimus, sequestribus metum inicimus,
divisores ratione aliqua coercemus, perfici
potest ut largitio nulla sit aut nihil valeat.

58. Haec sunt quae putavi non melius
scire me quam te sed facilius his tuis occu-
pationibus conligere unum in locum posse
et ad te perscripta mittere. Quae tametsi ita
sunt scripta ut non ad omnis qui honores
petant sed ad te proprie et ad hanc petitio-
nem tuam valeant, tamen tu si quid mutan-
dum esse videbitur aut omnino tollendum
aut si quid erit praeteritum velim hoc mihi
dicas; volo enim hoc commentariolum petitionis haberi omni ratione perfectum.

57. Thus if you are alert as this campaign demands, if you inspire your supporters, if you choose the right men to work with you, if you threaten your opponents with criminal charges, create fear among their agents, and restrain those who hand out their money, you can overcome bribery or at least minimize its effects.

58. That is all I have to say, my brother. It is not that I know more about politics and elections than you, but I realize how busy you are and I thought I could more easily set out these simple rules in writing. Of course, I would never say that these precepts apply to everyone seeking political office—they are meant just for you—but I would appreciate it if you have any additions or suggestions just in case, for I want this little handbook on elections to be complete.

THE RESULTS OF THE ELECTION

Marcus Cicero won the race for consul, gaining more votes than any other candidate. Antonius narrowly beat Catiline for the other consular seat. Catiline ran again the next year, but was once again defeated, prompting him to conspire to raise an army to violently overthrow the republic. In his role as consul, Cicero uncovered the conspiracy and persuaded the Senate to declare war on Catiline, who was subsequently killed in battle. For his actions, Cicero was named *Pater Patriae* ("Father of His Country"), a title he proudly bore the rest of his life as he struggled to preserve the power of the Senate against the rise of generals and dictators.

Quintus was elected praetor two years after his brother was chosen as consul. He served as Roman governor in Asia (modern Turkey) for three years, receiving long letters of advice from Marcus who remained in Rome. Quintus later served as a brave and capable lieutenant of Julius Caesar during the Gaulish War, though he turned against Caesar and backed Pompey in the subsequent civil war. Caesar pardoned him, but Mark Anthony and Octavian were not so forgiving when they came to power after the Ides of March. In 43 BC, Quintus and his brother Marcus were murdered as the republic itself died and the Roman Empire rose in its place.

GLOSSARY

ANTONIUS: Gaius Antonius Hybrida; a former henchman of the dictator Sulla, expelled from the Senate in 70 BC. Four years later, Cicero helped him be elected praetor, but in the consular election of 64 he allied himself with Catiline.

BUSINESS COMMUNITY: Latin *equites*; men of the second rank behind senators. This disparate group was usually more interested in money than in politics. It could, however, be influential in elections when it saw a threat to stability and freedom to make a profit. Cicero came from this order and relied heavily on its support.

CATILINE: Lucius Sergius Catilina; a supporter of Sulla, he had served as praetor four years earlier, followed by a notoriously corrupt term as governor in North Africa.

CENSORS: Two senior magistrates who regulated membership in the Senate, removing those members they deemed guilty of illegal or immoral activity.

CENTURIES AND TRIBES: Voting divisions of Roman citizens in elections.

CONSULS: Two were elected annually to serve as the chief civil and military officers of the Roman Republic. Membership in this elite and jealously guarded fraternity made a man and his descendants part of the Roman nobility.

CORNELIUS: Gaius Cornelius; served as tribune in 67 BC and passed laws to limit the power of the Senate. He was prosecuted in 65, but was successfully defended by Marcus Cicero.

COTTA: Gaius Aurelius Cotta; distinguished orator who backed Sulla and became consul in 75 BC.

DEMOSTHENES: The greatest orator of ancient Greece (384–322 BC), he overcame poverty and a speech impediment to rise to power. He was a hero and role model for Marcus Cicero.

EPICHARMUS: A Greek writer of comedy in the fifth century BC.

FORUM: Generally, an open marketplace at the center of any Roman town. The Forum of Rome was the focus of the city's political as well as business life.

FRIENDS: Latin *amici*; the term has a broad meaning, including political allies based on mutual interest as well as true friends.

GAIUS COELIUS: Tribune in 107 BC, he was the first of his family to achieve the office of consul, in 94 BC.

ITALIAN TOWNS: Latin *municipia*; these were self-governing communities with Roman citizenship. Cicero came from one such town.

MANILIUS: Gaius Manilius was elected tribune for 66 BC. He sponsored a law popular with the Roman people distributing freed slaves among the voting tribes, though it was soon annulled by the Senate. He was an ally of Pompey and conferred on him supreme command against the Asian king Mithridates and Mediterranean pirates. He was prosecuted by Pompey's enemies, but Marcus Cicero as praetor delayed the case as a favor.

MARCUS MARIUS: Nephew of the famous general Gaius Marius, he served as a praetor in 85 BC and announced plans to reform coinage. Popular with the common people, he was murdered by his brother-in-law Catiline in front of the tomb of Quintus Lutatius Catulus, a bitter enemy of Gaius Marius.

NOBILITY: Latin *nobiles*; men who had held the consulship or whose ancestors had achieved the office. They were the aristocratic rulers of the Roman Republic.

ORGANIZATIONS: Latin *sodalitates*; like the *collegia*, they were social or religious groups, but the term was also used for electioneering gangs who used violence to promote their favorite candidates.

OUTSIDER: Latin *novus homo* ("new man"); one whose ancestors had not previously held the consulship. Such men often held one of the lesser offices of state, but to serve as consul was rare.

PLATO: Greek philosopher (429–347 BC) who believed that a more real and lasting world lay behind mere appearances.

POMPEY: Gnaeus Pompeius Magnus (106–48 BC); a successful Roman general of great wealth and popularity among the general public.

PRAETOR: A Roman magistrate second only to a consul in power and prestige.

PUBLIC CONTRACTS: Those holding these were the *publicani*, businessmen who bid for contracts at auction, including tax collection. They became very wealthy and rose to great power in the Roman Republic.

POPULISTS: Latin *populares*; men who used the popular assemblies to pass legislation and gather political support from the masses. The difference between the *populares* and the traditionalist *optimates* was primarily one of means, not ideology, as both wanted power above all.

SPECIAL INTEREST GROUPS: Latin *collegia*; these could be occupational guilds, but also social clubs or political organizations. They held great informal power and sometimes used violence to protect their interests.

SULLA: Lucius Cornelius Sulla (138–78 BC); Roman dictator who legalized murder through proscription lists of those he deemed enemies of the state.

TRADITIONALISTS: Latin *optimates*; those who wished above all else to preserve the status quo, especially the power and privileges of the Senate.

TRIBUNES OF THE PEOPLE: Also known as the tribunes of the plebs, their duty as magistrates was to protect the lives and property of the common people. They could overturn an act by a magistrate or assembly with the word *veto* ("I forbid").

FURTHER READING

Alexander, Michael C. "The *Commentariolum Petitionis* as an Attack on Election Campaigns." *Athenaeum* 97 (2009): 31–57, 369–95.

Bailey, D. R. Shackleton, ed. and trans. *Cicero.* Loeb Classical Library 28. Cambridge, MA: Harvard University Press, 2002.

Boatwright, Mary, Daniel Gargola, and Richard Talbert. *The Romans: From Village to Empire.* New York: Oxford University Press, 2004.

Everitt, Anthony. *Cicero: The Life and Times of Rome's Greatest Politician.* New York: Random House, 2003.

Freeman, Philip. *Julius Caesar*. New York: Simon and Schuster, 2008.

Goldsworthy, Adrian. *Caesar: The Life of a Colossus*. New Haven, CT: Yale University Press, 2008.

Gruen, Erich. *The Last Generation of the Roman Republic*. Berkeley and Los Angeles: University of California Press, 1995.

Purser, L. C., ed. *M. Tulli Ciceronis, Epistulae*. Vol. 3. Oxford: Clarendon Press, 1953.

Richardson, J. S. "The *Commentariolum Petitionis*." *Historia* 20 (1971): 436–42.

Scullard, H. H. *From the Gracchi to Nero: A History of Rome from 133 BC to AD 68*. New York: Routledge, 1982.

Syme, Ronald. *The Roman Revolution*. Oxford: Oxford University Press, 2002.

Taylor, D. W., and J. Murrell, trans. *A Short Guide to Electioneering*. LACTOR 3. London: London Association of Classical Teachers, 1994.

Wiseman, T. P., ed. *Classics in Progress*. Oxford: Oxford University Press, 2006.